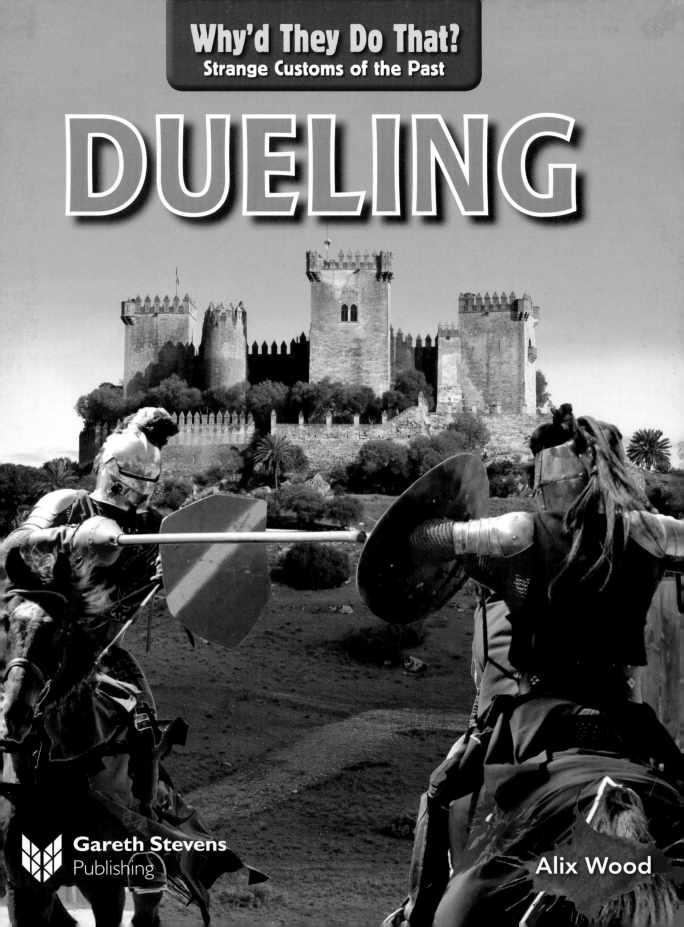

Why'd They Do That?
Strange Customs of the Past

DUELING

Gareth Stevens
Publishing

Alix Wood

Please visit our website, **www.garethstevens.com**. For a free color catalog of all our high-quality books, call toll free 1-800-542-2595 or fax 1-877-542-2596

Library of Congress Cataloging-in-Publication Data

Wood, Alix.
Dueling / by Alix Wood.
  p. cm. — (Why'd they do that? strange customs of the past)
Includes index.
ISBN 978-1-4339-9577-4 (pbk.)
ISBN 978-1-4339-9578-1 (6-pack)
ISBN 978-1-4339-9576-7 (library binding)
1. Dueling—Juvenile literature. I. Wood, Alix. II. Title.
CR4575.W66 2014
394.8—dc23

First Edition

Published in 2014 by
Gareth Stevens Publishing
111 East 14th Street, Suite 349
New York, NY 10003

© Alix Wood Books

Produced for Gareth Stevens by Alix Wood Books
Designed and illustrated by Alix Wood
Picture and content research: Kevin Wood
Editor: Eloise Macgregor
Consultant: Rupert Matthews, the History Man

Photo credits:
Cover, 1, 3, 4 top, 5 bottom, 7, 8, 9, 10 top, 14, 15, 16, 17 center, 19, 20, 23, 26 bottom, 27, 28, 29 top © Shutterstock; 4 bottom © Walters Art Mueum; 5 top © Nfutvd; 10 bottom © Public Domain; 11 top © Library of Congress; 13 top © Oscar Halling; 17 left and right © Public Domain; 21 © Library of Congress; 21 bottom © nga; 22 © 20th Century Fox/The Kobal Collection; 24 © Artothek; 25 top © Public Domain; 25 bottom © Sunset Boulevard/Corbis; 26 top © Public Domain; 29 bottom © C. J. von Dühren

Printed in the United States of America

CPSIA compliance information: Batch #CS13GS: For further information contact Gareth Stevens, New York, New York at 1-800-542-2595.

Contents

What Is a Duel?

A duel is a contest using deadly weapons arranged between two people in order to settle an argument. It is a very controlled sort of fight. The two people must fight on equal terms and follow an agreed set of rules, at a set time and place. The word "duel" comes from the Latin term *duellum*, a word made up of *duo* (two) and *bellum* (war).

Usually in a duel, one person would issue a **challenge** to another. Most duels occurred because someone had offended someone else's **honor**. An apology could stop a duel if it was done properly. At a duel, the duelists would each bring along a friend called a "second" to help prepare their weapons and make sure the rules of the duel were followed. If a man was confident in his own skill at dueling, it was the solution to virtually any problem. Debts could be erased by killing off the person to whom money was owed, and rivals for jobs or women could be wiped out, too!

This painting by Jean-Léon Gérôme is called The Duel After the Masquerade. *A masquerade is a fancy dress party; that's why they are wearing strange clothes!*

4

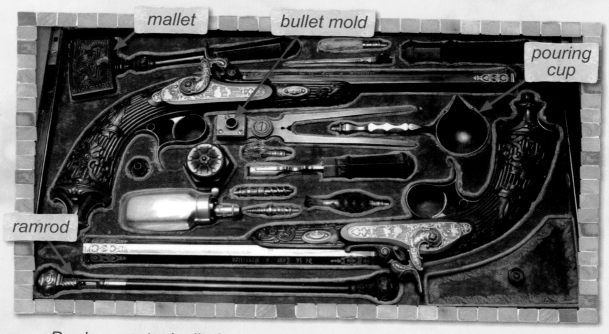

mallet

bullet mold

pouring cup

ramrod

Duels were typically fought with swords or pistols. Dueling pistols were sold in identical pairs, to make the duel as fair as possible.

Guns were a bit more complicated to fire then than they are now. Dueling pistols like the ones above came in a box with all the accessories you would need. You could even make your own bullets! Just heat some lead using the pouring cup and pour it into the bullet mold, then wait for it to cool. The mallet was for tapping the bullets into the barrel of the gun. The ramrod was used to push the bullet further down into the barrel. There were little flasks for the gunpowder, and plenty of tools for cleaning out the guns between uses.

RAMRODS

Your ramrod was very important. To prepare your ramrod when you first got your pistols, you had to push it into the empty barrel and mark the rod with a line where it stopped. Then you loaded a bullet and did the same again. You would now have two marks on your rod, one at loaded and one at empty so you could always quickly check if your gun was loaded.

How Do You Duel?

There were usually rules for conducting duels. In 1777, a committee of Irishmen drew up the dueling code that became widely used throughout Europe and America. The code was called the "Code Duello." The U.S. Navy included the Code Duello in its midshipman's handbook up until dueling by naval officers was finally banned in 1862.

A duel could be fought to a number of conclusions: to first blood, even if the wound was minor; until one man was wounded so that he could not continue; or to the death. The offended party could stop the duel at any time if he decided his honor had been satisfied.

In pistol duels, each party would fire one shot. Even if neither man was hit, if the challenger stated that he was satisfied the duel would be declared over. If the challenger was not satisfied, the duel may continue until one man was wounded or killed. More than three exchanges of fire was considered barbaric. Sometimes one or both parties would intentionally miss. This was known as **"deloping."** It often occured even though it was banned by rule 13 of the Code Duello: "no dumb shooting or firing in the air is admissible."

BACK TO BACK

For a pistol duel, the pair would stand back to back with loaded weapons in hand and walk a set number of paces, turn to face each other, and shoot. Typically, the worse the insult, the fewer the paces agreed upon. Sometimes a pre-agreed length of ground would be measured out by the seconds and marked out. At a given signal, often the dropping of a handkerchief, the opponents could fire. This reduced the possibility of cheating by turning around too soon. Another system had alternate shots being taken, with the challenged person firing first.

REALLY?

Any weapon could be used, and usually the choice was made by the challenged person. For many centuries, the choice was limited to certain types of swords. The loser of a duel was at the mercy of the winner. They could choose to spare the loser's life or kill him. The winner also had the right to do what he wished with the body of his rival. Often that would mean cutting off his head and displaying it in public!

In a sword duel, the swords had to be of equal length, with no sharp edges or notches. Usually the duelists needed to show that they were not wearing any defensive armor under their shirts. These armored knights look evenly matched, though.

Codes of Honor

A duel is not a brawl, it is a controlled battle between gentlemen of honor. A certain level of dignity was expected from the participants. Codes which regulated dueling ensured that the rules were followed, there was medical care at hand, and there were people present to witness the duel.

A copy of the Code Duello, known as "the twenty-six commandments," was usually kept in a pistol case for reference in case a dispute arose regarding procedure. The dueling site was referred to as "the field of honor." At the field of honor, each side would bring a doctor and seconds. The seconds would act as go-betweens to attempt to settle the dispute with an apology. If this succeeded, the dispute was considered to be honorably settled, and everyone went home. The code encouraged duelists to sleep on their wounded pride. They might reconsider the next day, or at least duel with a calm head.

REALLY?

In medieval Europe, dueling was a sport for noblemen. Swords were expensive so not everyone could afford one. Many countries had laws forbidding commoners to fight amongst themselves, while dukes, princes, and even kings were expected to duel.

THROW DOWN THE GAUNTLET

A challenge would often be called "throwing down the gauntlet." The phrase comes from medieval times. A knight would challenge a fellow knight or enemy to a duel by throwing one of his gauntlets on the ground. The opponent would pick up the gauntlet to accept the challenge. In more modern times, a dueling challenge was made by throwing a glove down in front of a person. It was then acceptable for that person to slap his challenger across the face!

Places chosen as fields of honor were usually isolated to avoid discovery and interruption by the authorities. Locations that were on the border of two **jurisdictions** or islands in rivers between two jurisdictions were popular. Uncertainty about which region's law applied there meant the duelists could avoid legal consequences.

Duels traditionally took place at dawn. The poor light would make the duelists less likely to be seen. Swordsmen dueling at dawn often carried lanterns to see each other.

Sword-fighting manuals even integrated lanterns into their lessons, using them to parry blows and blind the opponent!

Seconds

Seconds had an important role to play during a duel. They would find a suitable field of honor, and check that the weapons were equal and that the duel was fair. In the 1500s and early 1600s, it was normal practice for the seconds to fight each other as well! Later the seconds' role became more specific, to make sure the rules were followed and to try to achieve reconciliation.

When seconds disagreed and decided to exchange shots themselves, it had to be at the same time and at right angles with the main duelists. Seconds were also supposed to try to defuse the situation that led to the duel by getting an apology from one party or another. Sometimes there were thirds and fourths along for the fight as well.

A duel would often be observed by the principals' seconds, thirds, and often a medical man on each side as well.

Duel Fixing

Seconds have been known to fix duels for their friend's safety. During Britain's struggle against the French leader Napoleon, Prime Minister William Pitt the Younger chose to risk his life in an absurd duel. His plans to strengthen the navy had been criticized in Parliament by George Tierney. Pitt called Tierney a traitor and challenged him to a duel. Pitt's friend, Henry Addington, the Speaker of the British Parliament, chose to attend as a witness. At 12 paces, both men fired twice and fortunately missed twice. Some have hinted that the seconds deliberately loaded insufficient gunpowder to avoid a fatal injury. Pitt went on to lead the war effort against Napoleon.

A political cartoon showing William Pitt the Younger kicking his friend and political rival Henry Addington out of the door

Being a second could certainly be dangerous. US President Andrew Jackson was a survivor of several duels, but he nearly got killed when he was merely a second. One of the principals, Jesse Benton, was shot in the buttocks. He was angry at Jackson for his handling of the duel, and so was his brother, Thomas Hart Benton. Jackson threatened to horsewhip Thomas and went to a local hotel to carry out his threat. When Thomas reached for what Jackson thought was his pistol, Jackson drew his. Jesse burst through the door and shot Jackson in the shoulder. Jackson fired at Thomas, and Thomas shot back. At this point, several other men rushed into the room and Jesse was stabbed. He was saved from death by a coat button! A friend of Jackson's fired at Thomas who fell backward down a flight of stairs.

Avoiding Action

Often on the day of the duel, one or both of the parties would get cold feet. There were several ways to avoid having to take part and still leave with honor intact. Since the holding of the duel itself would usually be enough to satisfy honor, duelists might use **dummy bullets**, or declare ahead of time that they would fire their weapon into the air or at a non-vital area of their opponent's body.

In a sword duel, a son could fight on behalf of his father if the father was too old to defend an insult, or if there was too big an age gap between the two. The son could not duel for his father if the father was the challenger, though. This rule was designed to stop people offending each another, and then sending a strong, healthy substitute to fight on their behalf. In this case, the duel could be halted in the usual way by a sincere apology from the elderly man.

If this elderly man issues the challenge, his son will not be able to fight on his behalf.

Match Throwing

Delope means "throwing away" in French. Deloping is the practice of throwing away the first shot in a duel, in an attempt to stop the conflict. It was forbidden in the Irish Code Duello. Usually the deloper must first allow his opponent the opportunity to fire. A delope would be useful for practical reasons, for instance if the opponent was a better shot, or for **moral** reasons such as if the duelist did not want to kill his opponent. If the opponent insisted on a second shot after a delope, that was considered bloodthirsty and ungentlemanly. Often, the seconds would end the duel immediately after a delope had been fired.

REALLY?

Author and poet Edgar Allan Poe once managed to avoid a duel he had initiated with a newspaper editor by drinking too much beforehand to shoot straight.

In a duel, the **challengee** usually chose the weapons. One excellent way to avoid dueling was to choose weapons that were either ridiculous or obviously suicidal. **Howitzers**, sledgehammers, forkfuls of pig dung, and cat urine have been chosen as weapons! A sea captain and ex-whaler was challenged to a duel after the captain punched another man during a card game. The captain told the man's second that his choice of weapons was to be whale harpoons at twenty paces. The ex-whaler demonstrated how to use the harpoon by splintering a tree in his backyard. The challenge was quickly dropped!

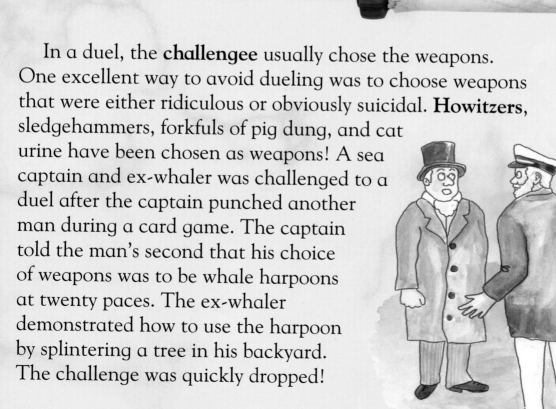

Strange Duels

There were many very inventive and bizarre duels fought over history. In 1843, two Frenchmen fought a duel by throwing billiard balls at each other! They drew straws for the right to throw first, then the two men stood 12 paces apart and took turns throwing the balls at each other. The winner hit his opponent on the forehead, killing him instantly. The victor wasn't able to celebrate his win for very long, however, because he was arrested and tried for murder.

In France, one of the more bizarre duels took place between a colonel named Barbier-Dufai and a royal guard named Raoul de Vere. The colonel insulted the royal guard's regiment badge on his hat! They started fighting with swords but after easily disarming Raoul four times, Barbier-Dufai saw a coach and horses pull up and thought up a more exciting plan. The two men decided to get into the back of the coach with their left arms tied together and fight each other with daggers, stabbing at each other in the confined space. After the carriage had done two laps around the Place du Carrousel, Raoul was dead and Barbier-Dufai was mortally wounded.

THE NINETEEN-YEAR DUEL

Captain Fournier loved dueling. When Captain Dupont tried to stop Fournier from attending a party, Fournier challenged Dupont to a duel. Dupont chose swords, and they fought the first of their 17 duels. Fournier stabbed Dupont in the shoulder. Dupont demanded a rematch, and this time Fournier was injured. Not content with a draw, they fought again and were both injured. They agreed to a pact that if they came within 100 miles of each other, they must duel, and they did, 13 more times! Eventually Dupont wanted to marry and didn't want to be engaged in regular mortal combat. He organized one final duel, this time with guns, even though Fournier was a better marksman. Dupont hung his jacket on a stick to trick Fournier into emptying his pistols into the decoy. Fournier was at his rivals' mercy. Dupont didn't kill him, though, on the condition that they could stop dueling forever. They never fought again.

REALLY?

In 1808, two Frenchmen fought in hot air balloons over Paris. One was shot down and killed along with his second.

Two young love rivals fought an unusual duel near Mont Blanc, in France. The men selected a place where **avalanches** were common and agreed to take turns standing for a given time in the most dangerous spot! The idea was that when one was killed by an avalanche, the other could propose to the girl. For three mornings, nothing serious happened. On the fourth day, one of the rivals was knocked down by an avalanche, but wasn't hurt. Eventually their food ran out, and they went home to stock up. By this time the police had heard about their strange duel and threatened them both with imprisonment. The rivals eventually settled their difference by drawing lots!

Famous Duels

Prominent and famous individuals were especially at risk of being challenged to a duel. To decline a challenge was considered the same as a defeat, and sometimes regarded as dishonorable.

In Britain, dueling amongst the famous and noble was common. In 1598 the playwright Ben Jonson fought a duel, mortally wounding the actor Gabriel Spencer. In 1798 the Duke of York was grazed by a bullet along his hairline during a duel. Four prime ministers engaged in duels, although only two of them, Pitt and Wellington, were prime minister at the time.

REALLY?

In America, the writer and poor shot Mark Twain narrowly avoided fighting a duel with a rival newspaper editor. His quick-thinking second pretended Twain had shot the head off a bird with a pistol, and the rival backed down.

In 1754 a young George Washington argued with William Payne, who hit Washington with a stick. Expecting a duel, Payne was summoned to a tavern the following day. Instead, he found a table with a decanter of wine and two glasses. Washington apologized for the quarrel, and the two men shook hands. Washington went on to become the first president of the United States.

BURR VERSUS HAMILTON

The most notorious American duel was between notable Founding Father and former secretary of the treasury Alexander Hamilton and his political rival, the vice president of the United States, Aaron Burr. Burr had blamed Hamilton for his defeat in the presidential election. Hamilton was against dueling, but met Aaron Burr on the field of honor in Weehawken, New Jersey, on the morning of July 11, 1804. The duel was fought on the same ground where Hamilton's eldest son, Philip, had died in a duel two years before. The same guns were used for both duels, too.

Aaron Burr *Alexander Hamilton*

It is thought that Hamilton fired first, aiming high and missing Burr completely. Burr then aimed squarely at Hamilton's torso and returned fire. Hamilton fell, the bullet lodged in his spine, and he died the following morning. Hamilton had recorded in a letter the previous night that he intended to purposefully miss Burr in an effort to end the confrontation without bloodshed. Some believe that Hamilton wrote this simply to paint Burr as the villain. Murder charges were brought against Burr, but he was never brought to trial. The event brought a swift end to his career, though. He was deprived of his New York citizenship and forced into hiding. In later years, he was shunned by society and died **destitute** on Staten Island in 1836.

Even Stranger Duels

One doctor solved a dispute between friends Henri Delagrave and Alphonso Rivière by bringing four pills to their duel. Three of the pills were harmless, but the fourth contained a deadly poison. Each agreed to take a pill in turn. The first two pills had no result. The doctor made them swallow the remaining pills at the same time, and a moment or two later Rivière fell down dead.

Humphrey Howarth, a British member of Parliament, had a quarrel with the Earl of Barrymore. They arranged a duel for the next morning. Howarth arrived armed with a pistol and wearing just his underpants. This caused some amusement, but Howarth had been an army surgeon. He knew that gunshot wounds could be infected by dirty clothing being shot into the flesh by a bullet. In the end, both he and his opponent missed their targets!

REALLY?

Two rivals fought a duel by each sitting on a barrel of dynamite with a lit fuse. Whichever fuse burnt down first would be the loser. Luckily, both fuses went out before the flame reached the dynamite. The rivals were so amazed that they forgot their quarrel.

A revolting duel was fought in Mexico between an Indian settler and a rich cattle-owner. The weapons were butcher's knives. Each man was to have one of his fingers cut off in turn. The first to show any sign of pain was to be shot by the other. The Indian had the first cut and amputated the cattle-owner's first finger. The Indian then lost a thumb. Neither flinched. The duel went on until each man had lost four digits. The cattleman's second became so appalled at the unpleasant sight that he rather unfairly shot the Indian dead and ended the fight.

SAUSAGES AT DAWN

The German statesman, Bismarck, challenged politician and scientist Rudolf Virchow to a duel. Virchow chose the weapons, two large and apparently identical sausages! He explained that while they both looked identical, one was infected with deadly germs. He challenged Bismarck to choose which of the sausages he would like to eat and that he would eat the other. Bismarck immediately lost his appetite for dueling and withdrew.

A Spaniard and a German both loved the daughter of Holy Roman Emperor, Maximilian II. The emperor did not want them to risk their lives in a normal duel. Instead he promised the girl's hand to whichever man could wrestle his opponent into a bag! The two men fought in front of the whole court, and the contest lasted over an hour. The Spaniard finally lost, having been put fairly into the bag by the German. The German took the bag and its Spanish contents and laid them at the feet of the young lady, and they married the next day.

Dueling on Horseback

Dueling is closely related to the **jousting** competitions of the Middle Ages. Dueling codes may be related to the codes of chivalry practiced by noble knights. A joust is basically a duel on horseback. Formal rules required that jousting competitors were of noble birth.

When two knights approached each other at the beginning of a competition, they were required to raise the visors of their helmets, revealing their identities to one another. This helped make sure that only nobles were participating in the fight. This gesture is believed to have evolved into the military salute.

A reconstruction of a jousting competition

REALLY?

Nostradamus is famous for his **prophecies**. He predicted the death of a king in a joust. Henri II of France was killed when his helmet—the "golden cage" described in the prophecy—was pierced by a lance.

SAMURAI WARRIORS

The Samurai fought archery duels on horseback. They would ride at each other and shoot at least three arrows. The duels did not necessarily have to end in death, as long as honor was satisfied.

Jeffrey Hudson, a dwarf, popped out of a pie at a party for the King of England, Charles I. His wife Henrietta Maria was enchanted by him, and he joined her court. She called him Lord Minimus. Hudson was a proud man. A young officer called Charles Crofts insulted him, and Hudson challenged Crofts to a duel. The soldier thought he was joking and turned up armed with a water pistol. Hudson demanded a real duel with real pistols on horseback. Hudson being so small was a tough moving target, so he escaped unhurt and shot Crofts dead. After the duel Hudson was exiled, captured by Barbary pirates, and spent the next 25 years in prison in North Africa. He eventually escaped and retired to his home county of Rutland, where they still drink a beer named in his honor.

Queen Henrietta Maria with Sir Jeffrey Hudson *by Anthony van Dyke*

Petticoat Duels

Duels weren't just a gentlemen's game. Although not as common, there were, in fact, a number of duels between women. They were often called "petticoat duels."

The most famous of these female duels took place in England in 1792 at London's Hyde Park between Lady Almeria Braddock and Mrs. Elphinstone. Their genteel conversation had turned to a bitter dispute after a comment about Lady Braddock's true age. The ladies dueled first with single-shot pistols. During this exchange, Lady Braddock's hat was damaged. They then continued with swords until Mrs. Elphinstone received a wound to her arm and agreed to write Lady Braddock an apology.

Julie d'Aubigny, better known as La Maupin, was a French 17th century swordswoman and opera singer. Her father trained her to sword fight, and she later had lessons from a fencing master. To support herself and her husband, she performed at inns and taverns, singing and fencing, dressed as a boy. She did not wear trousers to hide the fact she was a woman; it was simply easier to sword fight in them than in frilly skirts. La Maupin was rumored to have dispatched an entire roomful of young noblemen who complained when she insulted a lady they were dancing with.

REALLY?

A French officer began living uninvited in a house belonging to countess Madame de Saint-Belmont, a young widow. She sent a polite note of complaint but it was ignored. Annoyed, she challenged him to a duel signing the letter "**Chevalier de Saint Belmont.**" The countess disguised herself as a man and met the officer at the duel. An excellent fencer, she knocked his sword away and said, "You are mistaken if you think you have been fighting with the chevalier. I am madam Saint-Belmont. I urge you to be more sensitive to women's requests."

PIRATE MARY READ

Mary Read had taken a job on a ship, disguised as a man. Her ship was taken by pirate John "Calico Jack" Rackham and the female pirate Anne Bonny. After Read told Bonny that she was a woman, Rackham became jealous of their friendship and threatened to cut Read's throat, so he was let in on the secret, too. Read fell in love with a man they took prisoner. When one of the pirates challenged him to a duel, Read held a secret duel a couple of hours earlier and killed the pirate before he could harm her man.

Book and Movie Duels

The drama of the duel is a popular theme in movies and books. Russian authors were particularly fond of duels in their novels. Chekhov wrote a story called *The Duel*. One of the most famous fictional duels of all is probably Onegin's duel with Lensky in Alexander Pushkin's *Eugene Onegin*.

The Russian author and poet Alexander Pushkin described a number of duels in his works. The poet himself was mortally wounded in a controversial duel with Georges d'Anthès, a French officer rumored to have been seeing Pushkin's wife. D'Anthès, who was accused of cheating in this duel, married Pushkin's sister-in-law and went on to become a French minister and senator.

A painting by Ilya Repin of the duel between Onegin and Lensky in Pushkin's story

DAVID AND GOLIATH

In the Bible, Goliath, the Philistine giant, challenged the Israelites to send a champion for a duel. Young David accepted the challenge. Armed with only his sling and five stones, he hurled a stone with all his might and hit Goliath on the forehead. Goliath fell, and David cut off his head!

David and Goliath

REALLY?

An early Steven Spielberg film called *Duel* was about a car being chased by a mystery truck. The whole film was shot in less than two weeks!

Duels feature in many books and movies. The contest and tension can be very exciting. Some of the most exciting movie duels include the fight between Luke Skywalker and Darth Vader in *The Empire Strikes Back* (1980); between James Bond and Scaramanga in *The Man with the Golden Gun* (1974); Rob Roy MacGregor and Archibald Cunningham in *Rob Roy* (1995); and Harry Potter and Voldemort in *Harry Potter and the Deathly Hallows, Part 2* (2011).

A scene from the film The Duelists *(1977) adapted from Joseph Conrad's book* The Duel *based on the 19-year duel between Fournier and Dupont*

Wild West Gunfights

The typical cowboy film scene of two men marching off ten paces and firing their six-shooters on a dusty street did actually happen. The American frontier period was a time when dueling was popular in America.

In July of 1865 in Springfield, Missouri, Wild Bill Hickok lost at cards to Dave Tutt. When Bill couldn't pay up, Tutt took Hickok's gold pocket watch for security. Hickok growled that if Tutt used the timepiece, he would kill him. When Tutt wore the watch, this led to a gunfight. Tutt's shot missed, but Hickok hit Tutt in the chest. He stumbled and fell to the ground dead. Hickok was arrested and tried for manslaughter, but he claimed self-defense. Three days later, he was **acquitted** of all charges. Tutt's gravestone at Maple Park Cemetery is marked with a carved pocket watch, playing cards, and pistols.

Years later Hickok was playing poker in Deadwood. He usually sat with his back to a wall, but when he joined the game the only chair put his back to a door. Jack McCall walked in and shot Hickok dead. The poker hand Hickok was holding had a pair of aces and a pair of eights, all black. The hand has since been known as a "dead man's hand."

Texan Duel

In 1887 in Texas, gunslinger Jim Courtright was running a **protection** racket for gambling dens and saloons in return for a portion of their profits. Well-known gunman Luke Short was running the White Elephant saloon and Jim was trying to get Short to use his services. The two quarreled, resulting in one of the most famous gunfights in western history. With Bat Masterson at Short's side, Courtright and Luke Short dueled in the street in one of the few face-to-face gunfights in the American West. Drawing their pistols at close range, Short fired first, blowing off Courtright's thumb. Courtright then attempted to switch his gun to his uninjured hand, but he was too slow. Luke Short shot him in the chest, killing him.

REALLY?

As guns became common, a major change in dueling occured. Buying a pistol was less expensive than buying a sword, and there was no need for expensive fencing lessons. Dueling was now for everyone, not just noblemen.

Modern Duels

Dueling fell out of favor by the end of the 1800s. Even in the 1700s, George Washington encouraged his officers to refuse challenges during the American Revolutionary War because he believed that dueling deaths of officers would have threatened the success of the war effort.

Under British law, to kill during a duel was legally murder, but the courts were lax in applying the law and were sympathetic to the culture of honor. A ban on dueling in the military was more rigidly upheld. This was to stop anyone challenging senior officers to duels, killing them, and gaining promotion. Dueling was also considered bad for discipline. The military did not want officers questioning orders with the threat of a duel. Some duelists began to practice the art for sport rather than honor. It became a contest, not to the death, but to a certain number of points.

REALLY?

In October 2002, four months before the US invasion of Iraq, Iraqi Vice President Taha Yassin Ramadan suggested US President George W. Bush and Saddam Hussein settle their difference in a duel! Ramadan proposed that the duel be held in a neutral land, with each party using the same weapons, and with UN Secretary General Kofi Annan presiding as the supervisor. On behalf of President Bush, White House Press Secretary Ari Fleischer declined the offer!

AIRPLANE DUELS

A dogfight is a form of aerial combat between fighter aircraft, like a duel in the sky. Dogfighting first appeared during World War I, shortly after the invention of the airplane. Manfred Albrecht Freiherr von Richthofen, widely known as the Red Baron, was perhaps the most famous German fighter pilot involved in early dogfights. He shot down 80 Allied aircraft! Enemy pilots at first simply exchanged waves or shook their fists at each other. Only small weapons could be carried on these early aircraft as they couldn't take off with much weight on board. Pilots would sometimes just throw bricks, grenades, or rope at each other's planes, hoping to damage them.

A replica of the Red Baron's plane

Baron von Richthofen

Glossary

acquitted
To be declared innocent of a crime or wrongdoing.

avalanches
Large masses of snow and ice or of earth and rock sliding down a mountainside or over a cliff.

challenge
To invite or dare to take part in a contest.

challengee
A person who has been challenged by another.

chevalier
A knight or chivalrous man.

delope
To fire a gun into the air in order to end a duel.

destitute
Extremely poor.

dummy bullets
Imitation bullets that have no explosive used for training.

honor
A person's good name worthy of respect.

howitzers
Short cannons capable of firing a shell in a high arc.

jousting
A combat on horseback between two knights with lances especially as part of a tournament.

jurisdiction
The power, right, or authority to interpret and apply the law; and also the limits or territory within which authority may be exercised.

moral
Relating to the judgment of right and wrong in human behavior

prophecies
Writings that foretell or predict events.

protection
Money extorted by racketeers posing as a protective association.

For More Information
Books

Dixon, Philip. *Knights & Castles (Insiders)*. Simon & Schuster Books for Young Readers, 2007.

Fradin, Dennis Brindell. *Duel! Burr and Hamilton's Deadly War of Words*. Walker Childrens, 2008.

Greeley, August. *Pistols and Politics: Alexander Hamilton's Great Duel (Great Moments in American History)*. Rosen Publishing Group, 2004.

Websites

The History of Dueling in America
http://www.pbs.org/wgbh/amex/duel/sfeature/dueling.html
Learn about many famous duels in American history.

Seven Most Famous Duels
http://newsonrelevantscience.blogspot.co.uk/2012/06/throwing-down-gauntlet-historys-7-most.html
Read about seven well-known duels from around the world.

Publisher's note to educators and parents: Our editors have carefully reviewed these websites to ensure that they are suitable for students. Many websites change frequently, however, and we cannot guarantee that a site's future contents will continue to meet our high standards of quality and educational value. Be advised that students should be closely supervised whenever they access the Internet.

Index